George Washington

Tom McGowen

GEORGE WASHINGTON

Richard B. Morris, Consulting Editor

Franklin Watts   1986   A First Book
New York   London   Toronto   Sydney

Photographs courtesy of:
The Bettmann Archive: pp. 4, 27, 39, 44, 49, 50, 59;
New York Public Library Picture Collection: pp. 13, 20, 32.

Library of Congress Cataloging in Publication Data

McGowen, Tom.
George Washington.

(A First book)
Bibliography: p.
Includes index.
Summary: Recounts the life of America's first
president, including his youth in Virginia, military
career, role in the formation of an independent nation,
and leadership of that new country.
1. Washington, George, 1732–1799–Juvenile literature.
2. Presidents—United States—Biography—Juvenile
literature. [1. Washington, George, 1732–1799.
2. Presidents] I. Morris, Richard Brandon, 1904–
II. Title.
E312.66.M34   1986 973.4'1'0924   [B]   [92] 85-29560
ISBN 0-531-10108-8

Contents

Dedicated to my niece,
Arlene,
who'd have been against tyranny
in 1776, as she is now

George Washington

Chapter

1

Growing Up

On an April day in the year 1789, a man put his hand on a Bible and swore as the nation's president to uphold and defend the Constitution of the United States. He was the first man ever to take that oath and the first man to be elected president under the Constitution. He was the man who had made it possible for the nation to *have* a Constitution and who had been in charge of the work that brought the Constitution into being—George Washington.

George Washington was born on February 22 in 1732 in the British colony of Virginia to a well-off, landowning family that had lived in the colony for seventy-three years. At the time of his birth there were twelve colonies in what was to become the United States, and Virginia was the oldest one, having first been settled by English colonists 125 years before. So, while most of North America was then a land of enormous wild forests or vast, uncultivated plains, in which dwelt many different kinds of the people known as Indians, George Washington was born into a part of it that was a quiet, cultivated countryside made up of comfortable, stately houses and broad, orderly fields of crops.

The family George was born into consisted of his father, Augustine Washington; his mother, Mary; and three older children from his father's first marriage to a woman who had died—Lawrence, thirteen; Augustine, twelve; and Jane, nine. By the time George was seven he also had two younger sisters and three younger brothers. At this time the Washington family was living in an eight-room house called Ferry Farm, on some of Augustine Washington's land on the Rappahannock River across from the town of Fredericksburg. Most of the work around the house and in the fields was done by slaves—men and women most of whom had been forcibly taken from their homes in Africa, brought to North America in slave ships, and sold to farmers and merchants in the same way that cows and horses were sold. Augustine Washington provided food, clothing, and homes for these people, but he did not have to pay them anything and they were considered to be his property in the same way that his horses and cows were. This was the way things were throughout Virginia and some of the other colonies at that time.

So, George Washington grew up as the son of a prosperous, slave-owning farmer with considerable land. At the age of seven, as was customary for boys of well-to-do families at that time, George began his schooling, which consisted of learning to read and write and do arithmetic. Arithmetic quickly became his favorite subject. Of course, he also was learning about farming and the sorts of things that had to be done to keep a large farm going. He developed a love for horses and soon became an expert rider.

When George was eleven, his father died. In his will, Augustine Washington left George some tracts of land, ten slaves, and Ferry Farm, where he was to live with his mother and the younger children.

George had always been tremendously fond of his oldest half brother, Lawrence, who was now a married man of twenty-four, living on a farm of his own nearby, and Lawrence became a sort of substitute father to the boy. Lawrence had been a captain in a regiment of American infantry (foot soldiers) and had military experience during a war that Great Britain had fought against Spain, and his tales of military life apparently greatly influenced George. Lawrence believed George would have a better future as an army or navy officer than as a farmer, and when George was about fourteen, Lawrence urged the boy to join the British navy (which then accepted boys of twelve to fifteen as officer-trainees, called midshipmen). However, George's mother firmly discouraged this!

Adventures
of a Young Surveyor

Somewhat disappointed, George continued his life as it was. He was now studying mathematics, which he enjoyed very much. Working with problems involving angles and triangles led to an interest in surveying, which is the art of using lines, points, angles, and triangles to measure off amounts of land. In the storehouse at Ferry Farm were some surveying instruments that had belonged to George's father, and George began to work with these. There were many professional surveyors in the colonies, where land was always being measured for dividing up and selling, and George got one of them to teach him the basics of surveying. The boy found that he loved this sort of work, and by the time he was sixteen he was a skilled surveyor, earning money doing jobs of surveying for people in his part of the colony.

Interest in this work put the idea of joining the navy far back in George's mind, and then something happened that drove out that idea completely. Through his brother Lawrence, George had become acquainted with George William Fairfax, the brother of Lawrence's wife, who, although a young man of only twenty-three, was a member of the Virginia House of Burgesses (representatives) and an important person in the colony. In the spring of 1748, Fairfax was going to lead a group of surveyors out into the western frontier region adjoining Virginia to measure off and divide up a vast area of land there that was owned by his father, Lord Fairfax. He asked George to come along and help out with the work.

It was a great opportunity for the boy. Not only would he be doing interesting, useful work that would add to his experience and skill, but he would also be having an exciting adventure out on the frontier, where he had never been. Hopefully, he asked his mother's permission to go, and to his surprise and delight she agreed. She probably realized what a marvelous opportunity this was for her son and must have felt that he could take care of himself, for although George was only sixteen, he was already a sturdy six-footer (1.8 meters, or m), considerably taller than most full-grown men at that time.

So, on March 11, 1748, George rode off on horseback to join the group of surveyors. A week later he found himself camping in a tent for the night, for the first time in his life. Before long he was feeling as if he were a true frontiersman. In his diary he

By the time Washington was sixteen, he was an accomplished surveyor.

described a typical evening meal in the wild, writing that he cooked his food on a forked stick over a fire, and used a large chip of wood from a tree as a plate. At times he tried to hunt his own food, mostly wild turkeys, but apparently didn't have much success. For nights on end he slept either in a tent or in the open beside a guttering fire. And almost every day he did some surveying work, often under difficult circumstances, in muddy, partly flooded lands or heavily wooded areas that made sighting through an instrument almost impossible. He was back home by mid-April, full of tales of these frontier experiences.

Sickness, Sadness, and the
Fulfillment of a Dream

In the fall of 1751, George and the rest of his family became badly worried about Lawrence Washington, who had a constant cough and was losing weight. Everyone felt it might be bad for Lawrence's health to spend the winter in Virginia, and it was decided he should go to a warm, sunny place for a time, to see if this would help his condition. His wife could not go with him however, as she had just had a baby, so George volunteered to go along and look after his beloved brother.

They went to the island of Barbados, in the Caribbean Sea. George fell in love with the beautiful tropical land, but on the 17th of November he began to feel pain in his body and soon had a raging fever. He had caught the disease known as smallpox.

Doctors have eliminated this disease from the world today, but in George Washington's time it was so common that almost everyone caught it at some point during one's life. Many people died from smallpox, but those who recovered from the disease were immune and could never catch it again. George was seriously ill, but by the 12th of December he had recovered and knew he was now safe from this danger for the rest of his life. However, both he and Lawrence thought he should go home, so on December 21, George was on a ship sailing back to Virginia.

Lawrence stayed behind in the warmth and sunshine, but his health continued to go steadily downhill. He had the dreadful disease tuberculosis, for which there was no cure in those days. He came back to Virginia in early summer, but he was a dying man, and by the end of July he had passed away. This was a bitter loss for George, because Lawrence had been like a father to him.

Lawrence had held the position of adjutant of the colony of Virginia, which was a kind of part-time military post that had the duties of keeping written records, writing orders, and assisting the commander of the militia, the colony's volunteer military force. George had really never quite gotten over his desire, as a young teenager, to be a military or naval officer, and now, at the age of twenty, he found that he was extremely interested in taking over the post that had been held by his brother. Although he had no military experience at all, he visited the governor of the colony and other officials, trying to persuade them to appoint him the new adjutant.

After a time, the governor decided to create four adjutant positions, one for each quarter of the colony, and he appointed George Washington as adjutant for the southern quarter. On February 1, 1753, George was sworn into his new post with the rank of major. He immediately began reading up on military tactics and the art of being a soldier. The military career of George Washington had begun.

2

A Taste of War

At the time George Washington became an adjutant, there were thirteen British colonies in the part of America that was to become the United States. They stretched in a row down the east coast, and along the western borders of most of them were sections of frontier wilderness that were also claimed as British territory— territory into which the colonies could expand. But a little farther to the west and northwest lay a vast area of land that had been explored by Frenchmen and claimed as French territory, where there were numerous forts manned by troops of the French army. In the summer of 1753 Governor Robert Dinwiddie of Virginia received the worrisome news that a large number of French troops had come out of French territory into a part of the frontier known as the Ohio country, which the British government claimed as part of Virginia but which the French felt belonged to them. The French soldiers were building roads and forts, and although they were still only at the edge of the disputed territory, it looked very much as if they intended to push on in and take over the whole Ohio country for themselves.

This was a very serious situation, the sort of situation that could easily cause a war between the two nations. However, the British authorities hoped they could settle the problem peacefully. Governor Dinwiddie wrote a letter to the commander of the French troops, pointing out that he and his soldiers were in British territory and demanding that they leave.

Hearing of this, George Washington set out on horseback in a hurry to Virginia's capital, Williamsburg, to see Governor Dinwiddie and volunteer to be the one to carry the letter to the French commander. This would mean a long, hard journey through the wilderness, but George was eager to do something that would add to his experience and boost his reputation as an officer. It was exactly the right sort of task for a young officer, and Dinwiddie agreed to let George do it.

He was given the letter at the end of October and set out at once on November 1, 1753. As he traveled toward the frontier he worked out all his plans and figured out what he would need— a skilled guide to get him to the French commander, a person who could translate French for him, someone who could talk to Indians, and, of course, tents, provisions, weapons, ammunition, etc. By the 15th of November he had found the men he needed, purchased all his supplies, and was heading into the wilderness with a very well-equipped expedition of six men plus himself. Even as a young man of only twenty-one, George Washington was already a careful planner who worked everything out in advance.

Military Adventures

On a cold, wet day in mid-December he and his men arrived at Fort Le Boeuf, French headquarters, and George delivered the governor's letter to the French commander, an elderly, one-eyed nobleman. The French officers treated George and the other Americans with great courtesy, but they let him know that they felt the Ohio country belonged to France, and it was obvious they were getting ready to move farther on into it. George also saw that they were trying to persuade all the Indians in the area, many of whom were very friendly to the British, to become French allies.

Four days later, with a letter the French commander had written in reply to Governor Dinwiddie, George and his men started back to Virginia. The countryside was in the grip of winter now, and the journey was difficult and dangerous. Once, George was shot at by an unfriendly Indian, and another time he nearly drowned crossing a half-frozen river. His men suffered frostbite and injury. He finally reached Williamsburg on January 16 and handed the French letter to Governor Dinwiddie. As George had suspected, the letter stated that the French troops were not going to leave the territory they had taken over, and hinted that if the British tried to push them out by force, there would be war.

Washington's report and the French commander's letter convinced Governor Dinwiddie that troops would have to be sent into the Ohio country, and forts built in strategic places to block the French. He ordered George and other militia officers to begin recruiting men to form a small army. To George's delight, he was promoted to lieutenant colonel and told that he would be second-in-command of this army.

But finding men who were willing to be soldiers turned out to be a slow, difficult task, and the governor grew more and more anxious as the weeks dragged on. Finally, he simply ordered George Washington to take whatever men he had available and march at once to the Ohio River to set up a defense against any advance the French might make.

George had managed to collect 120 men, and at the head of this troop he started out on April 2, 1754. From time to time, more soldiers and supplies, sent by other officers, caught up with him, until his force finally numbered 159 men. But as the days passed and the tiny army drew closer to its destination, it became obvious to Washington that he was too late. The army began to run into fleeing frontiersmen, who warned him that a French force of some 800 soldiers had already reached the Ohio!

A message came from Governor Dinwiddie, telling George that his commanding officer, Colonel Fry, was on the way with more men. Washington decided to wait until Fry arrived. But on May 28, a small group of friendly Indians came to the Virginians' camp with news that a force of about thirty French soldiers was encamped a short distance away. Washington immediately decided to attack.

A First Victory, a First Defeat

The soldiers and Indians crept through the woods and formed a ring around the French camp, hiding themselves behind trees and bushes. Then, Washington stepped out into the open and gave the command to begin firing. The bang of musket shots rang through the woods. The French tried to fight back, but they were surrounded, outnumbered, and taking heavy losses. They quickly surrendered.

So George Washington's first battle was a complete victory. But this little battle, in which ten Frenchmen and one American were killed, was actually the beginning of a long and terrible war. It was known in Great Britain as the Great War for the Empire and was fought in North America, Europe, India, and on the seas.

In America it was known as the French and Indian War—and George Washington, with his attack on the little party of French soldiers, literally started the whole thing!

Washington and his officers had reason to believe that the small French force had actually been spying on them and had sent a messenger back to the main French troops to let them know there were American soldiers in the area. Thus, Washington expected to be attacked at any moment by a large French force. The place where his men were encamped was not very well suited for defending against an attack; it was on low ground and there were woods around it where men could hide as they fired. But George had his men fortify the place as best they could, by digging trenches and putting up walls of logs and earth.

As days passed, he began to receive reinforcements. First, a number of Indians joined him, then came 184 more Virginian soldiers bringing supplies and some small cannons, and later a company of British soldiers arrived. A message also arrived, telling George that Colonel Fry had died and that George had been promoted to colonel and was now in complete command of the Virginian army representing the king of Great Britain in the Ohio country!

By the 16th of June the French had still not attacked. George decided to take a chance and move forward to a place he had seen on his previous trip through the Ohio country that he thought could be more easily defended. But halfway there, his army was met by a messenger from a friendly Indian chief, who gave him the unwelcome news that a French force of 800 soldiers and 400 Indians was moving toward him!

His army would be outnumbered by three to one. He ordered a quick retreat back to where they had started from; even though

Washington, lieutenant colonel in the French and
Indian War, reading prayers in his camp, 1754

it was a poor position, it was at least fortified and would give his men a small chance.

However, by the time the Virginians reached the fort, their Indian allies had all left, for to try to fight against such great odds seemed foolish to them. Now, Washington had only 284 men to stand against the French.

At eleven o'clock in the morning of July 3, the French and their Indian allies attacked. From behind trees, bushes, and rocks they poured a steady, merciless fire into the frail fort. The Virginians' losses began to mount, steadily. Then, in the late afternoon a torrent of rain began to fall. To fire a weapon in those days, a man had to pour gunpowder out of a container down the muzzle of his musket, and sprinkle a small amount of powder onto a tiny pan that faced upward on the back end of the gun barrel. In rain the powder instantly got wet and would not burn. Before long, Washington's men were no longer able to fire their weapons. They had no way to defend themselves if the French should decide to rush them.

A French voice called out, asking if Washington was willing to talk about surrender. George looked around. A third of his men were dead or wounded; the rest couldn't use their muskets. He had no choice. He agreed to surrender, even though he knew the entire Ohio country would now be in French hands.

Washington and his men were allowed to keep their weapons and march back to Virginia, but even so it was a bitter defeat for the twenty-two-year-old colonel, and he was sure it would be the end of his military career. However, things did not turn out as badly as he feared. The government of Virginia passed a resolution thanking Washington and his officers for their "gallant and brave behavior in the defense of their country," and most people seemed to feel he had done the best he could.

Partaking in a Disaster

But to Washington's great disappointment, it was decided to break the Virginia regiment into separate companies, which meant he would no longer have a regiment to command. He was told he could command one of the companies, but he would have to accept the rank of captain—a drop of three ranks. Washington was too proud to take such a demotion, so he regretfully resigned from the Virginia militia even though he very much wanted to remain a soldier. He went back to Ferry Farm and spent the rest of 1754 taking care of business and visiting friends.

In January of 1755, English general Edward Braddock came to Virginia, and within the next two weeks, two red-coated infantry regiments of the British army also arrived. To George Washington's delight he was invited to become a member of the general's staff (a small group of officers who assist a general to make plans, write out orders, etc.).

Braddock's plan was to march straight into the Ohio country and attack the fort the French had built where the Monongahela and Ohio rivers come together (where the city of Pittsburgh stands today). On June 8, the British force and some Virginian volunteers, about 1,500 strong altogether, began to march into the frontier lands. It was a long procession of men marching four abreast in a column, horse-drawn carts and wagons loaded with supplies, and rumbling cannons, also pulled by teams of horses.

It was a long, hard march, but on July 8 the army crossed the Monongahela River and was only 8 miles (13 kilometers, or km) from the fort, which the French called Fort Duquesne. The marching column advanced about half a mile (0.8 km) and reached a broad, open spot in the forest. Suddenly, a French force of about 250 soldiers and 600 Indians attacked!

The French and Indians spread out in a half-circle among the trees, firing into the front and sides of the column of British soldiers. The men at the front of the column tried to pull back, but more and more British were coming up from behind them, and all these soldiers trying to go in two different directions quickly became a confused, milling mob into which the French and Indians rained bullets. The British soldiers, jammed together and unable even to see their enemies among the trees, could not shoot back. The war whoops of the Indians shocked the British, who had never heard such sounds before. The soldiers began to panic.

British officers and men were dropping by the dozens. A bullet suddenly tore through Braddock's arm and went into his lung. He slid from his horse and fell to the ground. George Washington saw an army cart standing nearby, and he and another officer carried Braddock to it. Leading the cart horses, Washington managed to get the wounded general back to the river crossing.

Washington helped lead the shattered, retreating army to safety. During the retreat, Braddock died. The British force had lost a total of 977 men and had left all its cannons behind. It was a crushing defeat.

A Promotion, an Illness, and a Final Adventure

Eventually, what was left of the army got back to Virginia. By that time, Governor Dinwiddie was frantically trying to put together more troops to defend the colony, and Washington learned from some friends that Dinwiddie wanted him to lead them. At the age of twenty-three, he was now commander in chief of all of Virginia's military forces, with his old rank of colonel.

Washington plunged himself into the job of trying to build up and improve the Virginia forces. He was deeply concerned, because groups of the Indians allied to the French were beginning to make raids into the outskirts of the colony, burning farmhouses and barns and slaughtering people. There simply weren't enough soldiers to prevent this, and Washington found it was very hard to find men who were willing to be soldiers, while many of those who did join up, quickly deserted. By May of 1756 there were only 321 men in the Virginia regiment, which was supposed to consist of 1,000 men. By having forts built at several strategic spots, manning them with small forces of soldiers, leading small groups in search of Indian raiding parties, Washington managed to cut down the Indian raids somewhat. However, he began to feel there would never be any chance of doing what he believed was the only real answer to the whole problem: making another—but this time successful—attempt to attack Fort Duquesne and driving the French back out of the Ohio country. A French retreat would force their Indian allies back into the wilderness and make them stop their raids.

Things kept on this way throughout the year and into the next. But in the summer of 1757 Washington caught the disease known as dysentery and became so weak that doctors insisted he had to leave his duties for a time in order to rest and recover. It wasn't until April of 1758 that he was well enough to return, but it was during this period of illness that George met someone who was to become very important to him—a young widow by the name of Martha Custis.

A lot of things had been happening while he was ill. Another British general, Brigadier General John Forbes, had come to Virginia and was preparing to do the very thing that Washington felt was most important—make an attack on Fort Duquesne. Washington was glad to hear that he and his regiment were to be part of this attack.

The expedition, made up of about 475 colonial soldiers and an equal number of British regulars, started out in early September. However, when the army reached Fort Duquesne in late November, they found that the French had burned the fort to the ground and had left the Ohio country. The fact was, the French were losing the war and had begun pulling all their troops together in order to make a last stand in Canada. But in September of 1759 a British army resoundingly defeated the main French army in a battle outside the city of Quebec, Canada, and this was the death blow to the French. By September of the next year the French had surrendered, leaving Great Britain in full control of Canada and the frontier lands of Virginia and most of the other American colonies.

Chapter

3

Farmer and Politician

George Washington knew that the danger to Virginia was over once the French had burned Fort Duquesne and left the Ohio country. He probably realized that whatever battles might still be fought would take place far in the north and he would not take part in them. For him, the war was over in 1758, and he probably felt there was no longer any future for him as a soldier. He had tried several times to get a permanent rank as an officer in the British army, but had been more or less ignored (which probably made him rather bitter toward the British government). So in December he once again resigned from the military service of Virginia. Soon after, in January of 1759, he married Martha Custis, the young widow he had met the year before, who was extremely wealthy and was the mother of two small children, to whom George now became a fond stepfather.

During the previous year, while George was taking care of his duties as a soldier, his name had been put up for election to the Virginia House of Burgesses, and he had been elected. The House began its work for 1759 on February 22, the date of Washington's

twenty-seventh birthday, and he was there to begin his new career as a politician.

He was assigned to a committee that worked on business regulations for the colony, and while he seldom made speeches or created any new regulations, he paid close attention to the way the House of Burgesses worked and learned how best to get things done. He impressed many of the other politicians, both with his abilities and his appearance, for he was 6 feet, 2 inches (1.9 m) tall, and towered over most other men of that time.

The house called Mount Vernon, which had belonged to George's half brother Lawrence, was now vacant, because none of Lawrence's children were still alive and his widow had remarried and moved to her new husband's home. George arranged to take over Mount Vernon, and he and Martha now made it their home. It was badly run down, but George went to work to put it back into shape and turn it into a profitable farm, growing tobacco. He split his time between farm work and his work in the House of Burgesses.

In 1760 the king that George Washington had fought for, George II, died, and his grandson was crowned George III. Lawrence's widow died that year, too, so Mount Vernon now belonged completely to George. The farm produced an excellent crop of tobacco that year and the next one as well. In 1761, George was up for reelection and won by a large vote.

Washington and his wife,
with her two children,
at home in Mount Vernon

Thus, the years peacefully slipped by, one after another. But then came the year 1765, and the American colonies suddenly found themselves having a serious difference of opinion with the government of King George III.

Taxes, Troubles, and
a "Tea Party"

What happened was that a large number of British soldiers had been kept in the colonies in case of further trouble with the French or Indians, and this was costing the British government a good deal of money. So, a way was found to make the colonies pay part of the cost. The British Parliament passed a law called the Quartering Act, which ordered the colonies to provide quarters (rooms), candles, firewood, and other things for British soldiers. A second law was also passed, called the Stamp Act, which required stamps to be put on a great many things that people in the colonies had to buy. Each stamp cost a small amount of money, and the money from all the stamps purchased by colonists would go to pay for the cost of the British troops in America.

But the Quartering Act and Stamp Act made many colonists extremely angry. These were taxes, and the colonists did not believe the British government had a right to tax them without their consent, for there were no men representing the colonies in the British Parliament. Many colonists simply refused to use the stamps; and in some places, bundles of the stamps were seized and burned and the British officials distributing them were threatened and some were even beaten up. There was also opposition to the Quartering Act, especially in New York.

George Washington did not approve of such violence, but he did feel that Parliament had been wrong to pass the Stamp Act.

Together with the other burgesses of Virginia he voted to declare the Stamp Act illegal and unjust. Representatives of nine other colonies held a meeting, known as the Stamp Act Congress, in New York in October of 1765. They sent a letter to the king, declaring that the British government had no lawful power to tax the colonies without their consent. Altogether, there was so much trouble over the Stamp Act that Parliament was forced to repeal it (call it off) early in 1766.

But all this created hard feelings in England. Many Englishmen felt that the colonies should be made to pay for keeping British soldiers in their country. Parliament declared that it *did* have the right to tax the colonies, and duties were at once put on many things that were shipped from England to America, such as paper, glass, paint, and tea. Parliament also began to look for ways to punish the colonies for causing so much trouble. The New York Assembly, which was the government of the colony of New York, where there had been serious trouble over the Quartering Act, was ordered to stop meeting, and there were rumors that the Virginia Assembly, to which Washington belonged as a burgess, would be broken up. To Washington and many other colonials it seemed as if the British government intended to take away the colonies' freedom to govern themselves and simply turn them into British possessions. In a letter that Washington wrote to a friend in 1769, he said that it looked to him as if "the Lordly Masters in Great Britain" would be satisfied only when they ended all American freedom, but that no man should hesitate to *fight*, if need be, to defend his liberty.

Matters between England and the colonies slid from bad to worse. On December 16, 1773, citizens of the city of Boston had the famous "tea party" at which some of them, disguised as Mohawk Indians, dumped tons of tea from England into Boston Harbor rather than pay the heavy taxes on it. Washington heard about this on New Year's Day, 1774, but he did not approve of it and apparently thought it would only cause trouble. It did. People in England, even those who were friendly toward the colonies, were outraged. Parliament passed an act stopping all ships from going to or coming from Boston until the tea that had been destroyed was paid for. Of course, this meant severe hardships for the people of Boston.

Delegate to the
First Continental Congress

In the days that followed, Washington and many other Americans were grim and worried. More bad news came from England: Parliament had passed an act that took away the right of the people of the Massachusetts colony to govern themselves. This act, the act to close Boston, and several other acts passed by Parliament, become known as the Intolerable (unbearable) Acts. They had been passed to punish Boston and strengthen British authority in Massachusetts, but they posed a threat to all the colonies. It seemed clear to Washington that the British government had decided to take full control of the colonies and rule them as it pleased.

Washington and many of the other burgesses began holding meetings on their own, to try to find some way of solving the problem. They were in touch with leaders of the other colonies, and it was agreed to hold a convention of all the colonies in Philadelphia, to decide what to do. Washington was selected as one of the seven men to represent Virginia at the convention.

He traveled to Philadelphia with Patrick Henry and Edmund Pendleton. They arrived on the 4th of September, 1774, finding the city crowded with delegates from other colonies. Washington found that a great many people knew of him, remembering his accomplishments as a soldier.

The convention, known as the First Continental Congress, worked out a plan for all the colonies to simply stop buying anything from England and to stop selling anything there. It was hoped that this would be so bad for the business of British merchants that they would force their government to change its policies toward the colonies. A letter was also written to the king, explaining the grievances of the American people and asking him to keep his government from trying to take away the colonists' freedom. The Congress adjourned on October 26, agreeing to gather together again in May of the next year to see what had by then come of their resolve to keep Britain and the colonies together.

But throughout the colonies, many people felt, as Washington did, that things might come to war. Everywhere, men were forming military units, getting hold of weapons and ammunition, and training as soldiers.

Commander in Chief
of a Rebel Army

Winter passed and spring arrived. But with spring came grim news that many had been fearing. There had finally been actual fighting between British soldiers and American patriots known as "minutemen"—because they were ready to fight at a minute's notice—at the little towns of Lexington and Concord in a part of the Massachusetts colony. The soldiers had been sent to search for hidden weapons and ammunition, and the Americans had tried to stop them. Seventy-three soldiers and forty-nine minutemen had been killed, and more than a hundred more on each side wounded. George Washington read about this in the April 28 edition of the

Virginia *Gazette*, only six days before he was due to leave for the meeting of the Second Continental Congress in Philadelphia.

He was in Philadelphia on the 9th of May, and was quickly assigned to committees dealing with raising troops and getting hold of weapons and ammunition. He impressed other delegates with his appearance and his way of doing things. They began to talk about him, remembering his reputation as a soldier.

The British force that had fought at Lexington and Concord had retreated into Boston, and thousands of American patriots were gathered outside the city to keep the British bottled up inside. On June 14, the Congress voted to form all these fighting men into an American army and to provide a general to lead them. By unanimous choice, George Washington was named as the commander of that army.

Rather hesitantly, Washington accepted, telling the Congress that he really did not think he was quite good enough for the job. He also made it plain that he didn't want to make any profit from helping the colonies fight for freedom, so he refused to take the pay that went with a general's rank, asking only that Congress repay him, when things settled down, for any expenses he might have to pay out of his own pocket.

Washington truly did not think he was capable enough or experienced enough to command an army, but he felt that if all the other delegates had such faith in him, he could not refuse their

Washington taking command
of the Continental Army
in Cambridge, Massachusetts

wishes. He could only try to do his best. On June 23, 1775, at the age of forty-three, George Washington set out to take command of an untrained, inexperienced, poorly equipped army that was going to have to stand up against the greatest military power in the world.

Chapter

4

*Military Leader
of the Revolution*

Across the Charles River from Boston at that time rose two hills, called Breed's Hill and Bunker Hill. There, a few days after Washington was named commander in chief of the American army, the American and British forces at Boston fought a battle that became known as the Battle of Bunker Hill. American losses were 400 killed and wounded; the British lost over a thousand men. George Washington learned of this battle on his way to join the army, and exulted to hear that the American soldiers had fought off two attacks before they had been forced to retreat because they had run out of ammunition. This showed that American fighting men could stand up against the British "regulars," who were counted among the best soldiers in the world.

On July 3, Washington arrived in Cambridge, 2 miles (3 km) south of Boston, to where the American army had retreated after Bunker Hill. He immediately found a number of serious problems. The American soldiers were more like a mob than an army; they had no idea of discipline (obeying rules) and did just about anything they pleased. Many of them didn't have enough clothing or blankets because most of the army's supplies had been left on Breed's

Hill. Some men did not even have a weapon. Many of the officers really had no idea of what they were supposed to do. Worst of all, Washington discovered that the army had hardly any gunpowder; there was only enough for each soldier to fire about nine shots!

Washington threw himself into the task of solving these problems while at the same time trying to keep the British troops bottled up in Boston. But he lived in constant fear that the British would come marching out of Boston and attack before he could have the army ready for them. However, the British commander, chubby-faced Sir William Howe, was overcautious and did nothing at all, so as the weeks slipped by, the supply of gunpowder grew, the army became more disciplined and well trained, and Washington was able to breathe more easily.

But as summer gave way to autumn a new and even worse problem appeared. Many of the men in the American army had been allowed to enlist for only a few months, and their enlistment periods would soon be over. To his dismay, Washington learned that many men intended to simply go back home when their enlistments were up. This would make the army so weak that Washington wouldn't be able to dare risk it in a battle. He sent a message to Congress, urging it to try to find volunteers to take the place of men who might leave, and he begged the soldiers to reenlist and stay with the army. But by January 1, 1776, the American army was down to a little less than 10,000 men.

However, volunteers and some militia companies began to arrive in Cambridge, and by the middle of February Washington had about 16,000 men. He began to think about making an attack to capture Boston. By March 4 all his plans were made, and that night he moved his artillery onto high ground overlooking Boston and had it begin to bombard Dorchester Heights, the part of Boston where the British troops were stationed.

But the attack didn't have to be made. General Howe decided the Americans had grown too strong and their artillery was in too good a position. So Howe put all his troops aboard British ships anchored in Boston harbor and sailed away, leaving Boston wide open for the American army to come marching in.

A Near Disaster

But where were Howe's troops going and what did he plan to do? Washington was sure the Englishman was going to try to seize New York City, so he quickly started the army marching to New York. By April 13 the Americans had arrived and Washington was looking over the city, trying to decide how to best defend it against a British attack. The sound of picks and shovels was soon heard in parts of New York as soldiers worked to dig trenches and put up walls of earth.

However, Congress now ordered Washington to send a portion of his troops to join a force that was being organized for an attack on Quebec, Canada. Washington obeyed, but this left him with only some 8,000 men, and he did not think that would be enough to hold the city against the attack he felt would soon be made by the British. For it was now known that Howe and his troops were in Nova Scotia, to the north of New York, waiting for reinforcements that were coming by ship from England, under the command of General Howe's brother, Lord Howe.

The work of fortifying the city went on through May and into June. Word came that the attack on Quebec had been a disastrous defeat for the American force, and the British troops in Canada were now free to move down against the colonies. Then, on the morning of June 29, a large fleet of British ships was sighted heading toward New York. By July 2 these ships, carrying thousands of

GENERAL ORDER

Issued by General George Washington *in* New York, *July* 1776

"The General is sorry to be informed that the foolish and wicked practice of profane cursing and swearing, a vice heretofore little known in an American army, is growing into fashion. He hopes the officers will, by example as well as influence, endeavor to check it, and that both they and the men will reflect, that we can have little hope of the blessing of Heaven on our arms, if we insult it by our impiety and folly. Added to this, it is a vice so mean and low, without any temptation, that every man of sense and character detests and despises it."

G Washington

British soldiers and German soldiers that had been hired in various parts of Germany, were anchored in New York Bay.

The New York City of 1776 lay on Manhattan Island, with Long Island just across the East River to the east, and Staten Island to the south, across Upper New York Bay. Washington believed that Lord Howe would first try to seize Long Island and use it to make an assault on New York, so he had his men fortify a long row of hills on Long Island, and put about 12,000 men there. Meanwhile, there came the news from Philadelphia that on July 4, 1776, the Congress had voted to declare the colonies independent from Great Britain. The United States had been born.

The British did, indeed, land troops on Long Island as Washington had thought. Early on the morning of August 27 they attacked, pouring heavy fire into the Americans spread out on the hills. But by midmorning Washington learned, to his dismay, that this was actually a trick; the main British force had gone around the eastern end of the hills and was now coming up *behind* the American troops, threatening to surround them. Quickly, Washington began pulling his troops out of danger. Rain and a dense fog that settled over the island helped him, and by the night of August 29 he had managed to get all of his troops, except for some 1,400 that had been killed or captured, off the island by means of boats. He had lost the battle for Long Island, but he had saved his army.

In 1776, it seems that
soldiers who fought the
king's army did not always
use the King's English.

The Americans retreated into New York City, on Manhattan Island, and on September 16 the British came after them. After a few hours of fighting, Washington pulled all his men out of the city to the northern part of the island. When the British pushed forward, threatening to trap the American army on the island, Washington retreated to the mainland. He did not dare risk trying to fight an all-out battle, not only because his army was badly outnumbered but also because the American soldiers simply couldn't be relied on, yet. Hundreds of them had run away during the battle on Long Island, and thousands more had deserted since then. So, throughout October and November, Washington continued to retreat through New York and New Jersey, with the British following but never quite able to catch him. Finally, Washington took his men across the Delaware River into Pennsylvania, heading for Philadelphia. By now it was December, and with winter setting in, the British commander decided not to follow any longer, and pulled his army back to spend the winter comfortably in New York City. Washington's army went into Philadelphia.

Two Vital Victories

So many American soldiers had deserted that Washington was now down to only some 3,000 men. Things certainly did not look good, and many Americans felt their cause was hopeless. Washington feared that if the people of the United States didn't soon have at least a small victory to give them hope, the Revolution might just collapse. He decided to take a desperate risk.

Lord Howe had left small forces at a number of towns along the New Jersey side of the Delaware River, and the force in the town of Trenton consisted entirely of the soldiers the Americans called Hessians, who had been hired by the British in Hesse and other parts of Germany. On Christmas night, Washington took his tiny army in boats across the ice-packed river and attacked Trenton. He had made his plans carefully, and caught the Hessians by surprise. Cannons poured fire into them from one end of the town, and when they tried to escape through the other end they found cannons thundering at them there, as well. Thirty Hessians were killed, 900 surrendered and became prisoners. There were only 30 American casualties.

Four days later, Washington took his men across the river again. He wanted to prove that the victory at Trenton had not simply been luck, that the American army could inflict more than one defeat on its enemy. But now the British were on the alert, and a strong force under Lord Charles Cornwallis came hurrying to crush the Americans.

Washington was nearly trapped. His troops were encamped at Trenton, and Cornwallis caught them there. On the evening of January 3, the little American force was huddled on one side of a creek and the powerful British force was on the other side, waiting to cross over and finish off the rebels in the morning. Cornwallis was sure he had the Americans; they couldn't get past his army because the road across the creek was well guarded, and they couldn't retreat because the Delaware River was right behind them, so full of ice that boats couldn't cross it, but not solid enough for men to walk on.

However, that night Washington and his men left their camp-fires burning to fool the British and quietly slipped far to one side, around Cornwallis's force. They marched to the nearby town of Princeton, where they met another British force coming to aid Cornwallis, and defeated it in a quick battle, capturing a large quantity of much-needed supplies.

One of the greatest generals of that time, King Frederick (the

Great) of the German kingdom of Prussia, said that what Washington had done was one of the most clever military operations in history. The British were so astounded and worried about what Washington might do next that Howe simply pulled all his troops out of southern New Jersey—a retreat! The two little victories raised the spirits of many Americans who had nearly given up, while in England there was great concern.

The British commanders in England now hatched a plan to close around the rebel army and wipe it out. A British army under General Burgoyne was to come marching down out of Canada in June, and Howe was to lead his army northward to meet it. This would cut the colonies in half, block Washington's escape, and destroy his army.

But things got mixed up. Howe was never told exactly what to do, so he simply turned south and began trying to catch Washington himself. Meanwhile, thousands of New England farmers flocked to form an army under American general Horatio Gates, and Burgoyne began to find this army in his path at almost every step. It wore his force down with several battles, and finally surrounded him and forced him to surrender in October of 1777.

This was a turning point in the war. Many Americans who hadn't really thought the Revolution had much chance, now began to believe the United States could actually win. Burgoyne's defeat also convinced the French government that the rebels had a good chance of winning, and the French would rejoice to see their old enemy, England, defeated and humiliated. So, France, which had been secretly helping the Americans by supplying them with supplies and weapons, took the serious step of officially recognizing the United States as a new nation, independent of Great Britain—the first step toward actually helping the Americans to *fight* the British. There were also now many Englishmen who believed the rebels could win, and who were clamoring for the British government to stop the war and do everything possible to get the Americans to remain part of Great Britain.

A Winter of Suffering

But while American general Horatio Gates was scoring victories against Burgoyne, Washington was having a bad time against Lord Howe. Washington's victories at Trenton and Princeton had caused men to come flocking to join his army, but it was still outnumbered by Howe's force. When Howe came marching into Pennsylvania, Washington tried to bar his way, waiting for him on the bank of a creek called the Brandywine. But while part of Howe's army moved straight toward Washington's force, another part swung around and hit the Americans from the side. Washington lost 1,000 men and had to retreat back toward Philadelphia.

The streets of Philadelphia began to ring with shouts of "The British are coming!" Congress was still meeting there, but now the congressmen and their families hurriedly fled to avoid being captured. On the 27th of September, Howe marched into the city with part of his army, leaving the other part at the nearby town of Germantown. On October 4, Washington made a surprise attack on Germantown and pushed the British troops out for a time, but then the rest of Howe's army came hurrying from Philadelphia and most of Washington's men fled in panic, believing they were surrounded. Disappointed because he had felt he could recapture Philadelphia, Washington took his army to a region known as Valley Forge, 25 miles (40 km) from Philadelphia, to spend the winter.

The Americans endured a winter of suffering at Valley Forge. They lived in tattered tents and log huts they built themselves,

which barely kept out the worst of the cold. They had no winter clothes, and as time went on, the clothes they had began to wear out, leaving many men dressed in rags and some actually half-naked. There was never enough food, and smallpox and other diseases raged through the camp, killing weakened and underfed men by the thousands! Many men deserted. By mid-December there were less than 3,000 soldiers left. Washington did what he could, writing for help to Congress and governors, sending out groups of the healthiest men to look for food, trying to get hold of clothing and blankets. He made himself look calm and unworried when he went among his men, but secretly he was afraid the army was just going to melt away to nothing.

To make matters worse, Washington was now being personally attacked by some of the other men who had been appointed generals and by a number of congressmen. General Gates, who had commanded the army that beat the British general Burgoyne, apparently felt that he deserved to be commander in chief of the American forces rather than Washington. Gates sent his aide Colonel James Wilkinson to York, Pennsylvania, where Congress was now meeting, and Wilkinson did everything he could to praise Gates and blame Washington. As a result of all this, some congressmen started a move to have Washington replaced by Gates, but this was finally prevented by the other members of Congress.

Bas-relief at the Sub-Treasury Building in New York of Washington praying at Valley Forge

So, Washington weathered his storm and the army at Valley Forge weathered its storm, too. The men who stayed on and survived were the strongest men and the true patriots. All winter long, a former Prussian army officer, Baron Frederick von Steuben, taught them how to load and shoot faster and how to fight in formation as the British did. He turned the young farmers, clerks, and mechanics into soldiers, and by the time the ice had melted and the fields and trees had turned pale green in the early spring of 1778, the tiny American army was well-trained, well-disciplined, and confident.

Good News, a Victory, and a Troubled Siege

In May came the exciting news that France had signed an alliance with the United States, and on June 17 France went to war with Great Britain. The rebels now had a powerful ally!

The British troops suddenly left Philadelphia and began to march toward New York. Washington immediately followed, with an army that had now grown to 13,000 men. He caught up with the British in New Jersey on a sizzling-hot day. His plan called for Major General Charles Lee to attack the British rear guard with 5,000 men, and when the main British force turned to fight Lee, Washington would attack with the rest of the American army. But the British had barely begun to fight off Lee's attack when Lee called for a retreat. Washington was furious, and when he encountered Lee he spoke angrily to him. He then quickly moved his force into position to stand off the British, who had now launched a powerful attack of their own.

The Americans stopped the British dead in their tracks. Four times the red-coated regiments tried to push forward, and each time they were hurled back. Night fell, and under cover of darkness the British stole away, having discovered that this American army that had come out of Valley Forge was now their equal.

Washington moved on after the British. On the night of July 13 he received a thrilling message from Congress, telling him that a fleet of French warships had reached the American coast. When the British went into New York City, Washington took his army to White Plains, New York, just a few miles to the north.

By now it was autumn, and Washington, feeling sure the British would not come out of New York at least until spring, split up the American army among several nearby towns for the winter. It was a much better winter for the army than the last one had been—now, the troops had received new uniforms and blankets, and there was plenty of food. In December, Washington was called to Philadelphia to discuss the future of the war with members of Congress, and he was able to be with Martha, who joined him there. It was decided that, with the northern British army bottled up in New York, help should be sent to the south, where British forces controlled Georgia and were threatening South Carolina. Washington sent a small part of his army to the south, to link up with the southern American forces and French troops that were heading south from Boston.

Spring flowed into summer and summer into autumn. In November came the unwelcome news that a combined attack by French and American troops against the British in Georgia had failed. The south was still firmly in British hands.

Another winter arrived, and again Washington had to spend most of his time trying to keep his soldiers well fed and warm, for there had been a drought throughout the northern states, there was a shortage of flour, and few if any farmers were willing to sell food to the army for the paper money Congress had created for paying the soldiers. Things were nearly as bad as they had been at Valley Forge, and by the spring of 1780 it again seemed as if the army might just fall apart from lack of food and supplies. On the 25th of May there was actual mutiny, with soldiers threatening their officers with bayonets. The officers got the men calmed down, but Washington wrote in his diary that he had never been as worried about anything as he had been about this!

Provisions came dribbling in, but there were never enough. Things got so bad that when reinforcements came to join the army, Washington actually had to send them away—there simply wasn't enough food! He began moving the army about, going from a place where food was scarce to where it was more plentiful, staying as long as possible, then going somewhere else. While doing this, he also had to keep an eye on the British in New York.

It seemed as if things could hardly get worse, but in September 1780 Washington discovered that one of his most trusted and efficient officers, General Benedict Arnold, had turned traitor and joined the British!

Congress had sent General Gates south to take command, but Gates was badly defeated when he tried to retake Charleston. Congress decided a new commander was needed, and in October Washington sent one of his best generals, Nathaniel Greene, to take over the southern forces. Then he again split up his army among several towns for the winter. Food was still a serious problem, and mutinies flared up again in December and January. Washington wrestled continuously with the problems of keeping his army fed, holding it together, and also of somehow sending help to Greene in the south.

Final Victory

But now, the tide was about to turn. In the spring, the British commander in the south, Lord Cornwallis, hatched a plan to cut the north and south apart by taking over Virginia, and decided to use Yorktown, at the tip of the Virginia peninsula, as his base of operations because he could be supplied there from the sea by the British navy. So he foolishly crammed his army into the narrow area at Yorktown—like a cork in the neck of a bottle.

Learning of this, Washington realized that if the French fleet could keep the British fleet away from Yorktown, Cornwallis' army would be trapped there and could be destroyed. He quickly got in touch with the French commander, the Count de Rochambeau, and explained his plan. Rochambeau agreed and sent word to the French naval commander to sail to Yorktown. Leaving only 2,000 men to hold the British force in New York, Washington took the rest south, moving as quickly and quietly as possible, to try to keep the British from finding out what was happening.

The Americans arrived outside Yorktown on September 14, 1781, and found that everything had gone as planned. There had been a five-day battle between the French and British fleets, and the British had been defeated and had sailed to New York. The French had landed 7,800 men outside Yorktown, and Washington had brought 9,500 men. There were about 8,000 British trapped in Yorktown.

Under Washington's command, the French and Americans besieged Yorktown. For days on end their cannons kept up a steady bombardment of the British fortifications. French and American troops began breaking through the outer defenses. On October 19, Lord Cornwallis surrendered.

When news of this reached England, the head of the British government, the prime minister, resigned. A new government was formed, and on March 2, 1782, it officially asked the American government to discuss peace terms. The war was now virtually over.

Washington entering New York as hero a month
after the peace treaty with Britain was signed

However, Washington made sure the army was kept strong and well supplied, just in case fighting should flare up again.

On September 3, 1783, a final peace treaty was signed in Paris, and Great Britain officially recognized the United States as a new, independent nation. By December, the last British troops and ex-officials had left the country. On December 4, Washington called all his officers together, and there were tears in most men's eyes as they said good-bye to this man who had led them from days of dark desperation to this time of triumph. Washington then resigned as commander of the American army.

Chapter

5

Overseer of the
Constitution and the Nation

George Washington was now fifty-one years old and he was looking forward to days of peace and quiet and nothing to worry about, with his wife at their home in Virginia. During the next few years after returning to Mount Vernon he spent most of his time improving the plantation, searching for new land to buy, and taking part in several canal-building and land-improvement plans. But he continued to keep an eye on what was happening all over the country, and as time went on he grew more and more worried about the future of the United States.

The thirteen states still all had their own governments and were joined together in a kind of alliance called a confederation, which was rather loosely run by the Congress of representatives from each state, working with a set of laws known as the Articles of Confederation. But it had become obvious that this system was not working at all well. The states all operated like separate nations, each with its own laws, its own taxes, and even with different money, which made it hard for states to do business with one another. Things were often so confused and difficult that some people even felt it would be better to rejoin Great Britain! Washington, like many other Americans, feared that the new little nation might soon just fall apart unless something was done to create a government that would work for all the states together.

Early in 1787 all the states agreed to make an attempt to change the Articles of Confederation to make them work better. Each state except Rhode Island chose a number of delegates to meet together and work out the changes, and Washington was asked to head the group of delegates from Virginia. He really did not want to; he had not been feeling well, the plantation needed his attention, and he really didn't think the meeting would accomplish anything. But so many of his friends felt he should go that he finally reluctantly agreed.

The meeting was to be held in Philadelphia, and when Washington arrived there on the 13th of May, 1787, he was met by cheering crowds and ringing church bells. He was tremendously admired and respected by everyone. One of the first needs of all the delegates was to select a chairman for the meeting, a leader who could keep them on the proper path and guide them through difficulties. Washington was the unanimous choice.

The Birth of the U.S. Constitution

So, with Washington in charge of the meeting, the work began. The delegates from Washington's state, Virginia, offered a plan for a complete change of government. The proposed new kind of government would have a president, to provide leadership and direction; two groups of representatives from the states, to create needed laws; and a supreme court, to judge the working of the laws. Later, a delegate from New Jersey offered a plan to just change the Articles of Confederation by increasing Congress's powers without reducing the powers of the separate states. But this plan was voted down. The delegates went to work to put the Virginia Plan into a shape that everyone could agree on. It was to be a set of rules for governing a nation formed of a union of states—a Constitution for the United States of America.

The creation of the Constitution was completed by mid-September, and on September 17 the delegates voted to accept it. Washington had not actually contributed much to the ideas or wording that finally went into the Constitution; in fact, some of the things he wanted and voted for lost out. But simply by being part of the convention that put the Constitution together, Washington played an important role, for the Constitution now had to be ratified, or approved, by each state, and while there were many people who were not satisfied with it, it seemed that as far as most people were concerned, anything that George Washington had had a hand in was bound to be good! So, by June 21, 1788, nine states had ratified the Constitution, and that was enough to make it the official foundation for a new United States government. And, as James Monroe said to Thomas Jefferson, it was thanks to George Washington's influence that the country could finally look forward to a workable government.

But to his dismay, Washington now saw that because most people thought he had played such a large part in putting together the new government, they believed he should be the head of that government—there was an overwhelming desire for Washington to be the first president under the Constitution. Washington worried and fretted over what he should do if he were nominated for the job. He felt he had earned a peaceful retirement in his old age and didn't want to take on any new, unfamiliar duties.

Finally, after some time, his own conclusions and the opinions of many of his friends led him to decide that he must do what he

THE FOUNDATION OF AMERICAN GOVERNMENT

On September 17, 1787, Washington presided
over the signing of the Constitution.

could to make sure the new Constitution and the new federal government got off to a good start instead of possibly being crippled by those who opposed them. He decided that if he were elected president he would accept and serve.

The Nation's First President

There was never really any doubt. In February of 1789, George Washington was elected first president of the United States by all sixty-nine votes of the Electoral College. He traveled to New York City, which had been designated the capital of the new nation, and was sworn in on the 30th of April. His vice-president was John Adams of Massachusetts.

On the 1st of May, Washington plunged into the hardest work of his life. He believed that his duties should consist mainly of supervising the United States' relations with other countries and seeing that the laws and measures passed by Congress were carried out, but this resulted in many meetings with foreign representatives, long discussions with members of Congress, and hours of careful reading of bills, speeches, and reports. He did not feel that he should try to have anything to do with the passing of laws, but he believed firmly that he should try to stop the passage of anything he did not agree with, by means of a veto (the refusal to sign a bill voted by Congress, which keeps it from becoming a law).

On April 30, 1789, Washington was sworn in as the first president of the United States.

It was also part of Washington's job to pick the heads of various "departments" (Department of the Treasury, Department of War, etc.) that had been created by Congress to help run things, and on September 11 he appointed his trusted friend Alexander Hamilton, who had worked so hard for the Constitution, as secretary of the treasury. The next day Washington gave the post of secretary of war to General Henry Knox, who had been in charge of Washington's artillery during the war. Later in the month, Edmund Randolph was made attorney general, and Thomas Jefferson appointed secretary of state. Within time, Washington began calling these men together for meetings to discuss problems, and thus the tradition of a United States president's "cabinet," or team of advisers, was born.

One of the most important events of Washington's first four years as president was the passage of an act (law) to provide the first Bank of the United States. This was Hamilton's idea, but Washington favored it. Washington cast the first presidential veto in 1791, when he refused to sign a bill increasing the number of congressmen from each state. He felt this would give some states a greater, unfair representation in Congress.

It was during Washington's first four years that political parties began to form. A group led by Alexander Hamilton believed that a stronger national, or *federal*, government was needed, and they became known as "Federalists." Another group, led mainly by Thomas Jefferson, believed there would be more freedom and liberty if each state had greater control over its own affairs. This group called itself "Democratic-Republicans." For the most part, businessmen and people in the northern states favored the Federalists, while farmers and southerners leaned toward the Democratic-Republicans. Washington was careful not to show favoritism for either party; he was actually against the idea of political parties, fearing they would split the country.

Washington had intended to serve only one term as president and then retire back to Mount Vernon, and he even had James Madison start work on a farewell speech for him. But as 1792 began to draw to a close both Hamilton and Jefferson tried persuading him that he must stay on for another term in order to keep the nation together. Washington never formally announced that he would run for office again, but he didn't announce that he intended to retire, either—and so, in February of 1793 he was again unanimously elected.

A Troubled Second Term

At the beginning of Washington's second term the nation faced a great many more problems. There was trouble with Great Britain over some frontier forts that were still occupied by British troops; trouble with Indians, who were attacking American settlements on the frontiers; and trouble about France, which had become involved in a war with Great Britain and other European nations, and which, because France and the United States had signed an alliance in 1778, thought the United States should take its side. But the French government of 1793 was completely different from that of 1778; there had been a revolution in France, and the king who had sent troops and ships to help America had been executed! France was now a republic, like the United States, and Jefferson and the American Democratic-Republicans felt the United States *should* help it, while Hamilton and the Federalists insisted the United States should be neutral for its own good.

The trouble over France quickly worsened. In April of 1793, Washington had to ask the French government to take back the man who had been sent to officially represent it in the United States. This man, Edmond Genêt, had done everything possible to get the United States to take France's side. He had also bought some American ships, loaded them with cannons, hired American crews, and sent the ships out to attack British shipping; and he had even tried to organize armies of Americans to attack Canada. Of course, the British government was greatly angered by such acts, and there was serious danger that the United States might be drawn into another war with Great Britain.

In hopes of preventing this, Washington sided with the Federalists and issued a "Proclamation of Neutrality," officially announcing that the United States would not take sides between France and Britain or any of the other nations with which France was at war. This infuriated the Democratic-Republicans. Some of the American newspapers that favored their cause now began to print attacks on Washington for the first time, accusing him of betraying America's old friend France and of being so puffed up by his own importance that he had lost touch with the true feelings of the American people. Washington was hurt and angered by such attacks.

The troubles multiplied. The Indians in the Ohio country were in full warfare. Great Britain announced that its warships were going to stop any American ships heading toward France and seize their cargoes. A terrible epidemic of yellow fever broke out in Philadelphia, and more than 4,000 people died during the three months it raged.

Turmoil Over a Treaty

Thus, when 1794 arrived, Washington faced a host of problems. What still worried him most was the serious danger of a war with Great Britain. In the spring he sent Chief Justice John Jay to England to work out a treaty which, Washington hoped, would end all the problems between the two nations. On November 19,

Jay signed a treaty by which the British agreed to remove all their troops out of forts in what the United States regarded as American territory, in return for a number of agreements. But when the people of the United States learned of the treaty, early in 1795, there was a feeling among many that the United States had come out second best. The treaty had to be ratified by Congress, but it was bitterly opposed by the Democratic-Republican senators, who felt that it not only gave more to Great Britain but also actually helped do harm to France. When it was voted on, it passed, but only by the narrowest margin.

President Washington still had to sign the treaty before it became official, but he could not decide whether he should or not. If he signed it, relations between the United States and Great Britain would probably become much better and the danger of war would end—but *did* the treaty shortchange the United States and hurt its friend France?

Washington talked with his cabinet members and wrote letters to friends, trying to get help in making up his mind. But in the meantime there were riots against the treaty in Philadelphia and New York, and letters poured in to Washington from people who were against it. Edmund Randolph, who had replaced Jefferson as secretary of state, told Washington that people all over the country were up in arms about the treaty. It seemed as if Randolph felt it would be a bad mistake if the president signed the treaty.

By August, Washington had pretty well made up his mind not to sign the treaty unless Great Britain agreed to certain changes in it. But then, the president was shocked and stunned when one of his other cabinet members showed him apparent proof that Edmund Randolph, who had been Washington's trusted friend for years, was being paid by the French government to try to influence Washington against signing the treaty! Naturally it would be to

France's advantage if the United States and Britain could be kept apart and perhaps even forced into a war.

Saying nothing to Randolph, Washington called a meeting of his cabinet and again asked the members for their opinions on whether or not he should sign the treaty. Randolph argued strongly that the treaty should not be signed unless Great Britain agreed to changes. When he finished speaking, Washington stood up, and to Randolph's astonishment said, "I will ratify the treaty!" Even though the president actually agreed with what Randolph said, he could not let himself be influenced by a man who was apparently working for a foreign government. Several days later Washington showed Randolph the proof of his treachery, a letter from a French government official. Randolph protested that it was all a mistake, but he resigned as secretary of state.

So, Washington signed the treaty. The Federalists were delighted, but the Democratic-Republicans were enraged. Some of them attacked and insulted Washington in savage speeches in Congress. Some newspapers called him a "tyrant" (dictator), and others declared that he had shown himself to be stupid. As time went on, these attacks grew worse, and Washington was accused of all sorts of things—of having taken on the job of president for power and glory, of having falsely accused Randolph, and even of having been a poor general during the Revolutionary War!

However, it seemed as if most of the country was siding with Washington and was in favor of the treaty, and so, the attacks on the treaty and on George Washington finally died away.

Saying Farewell

But Washington had had enough. Seventeen ninety-six was the last year of his second term as president, and he had no intention of serving any longer. He made it known that he intended to retire when the term was up.

He gave a great deal of thought to how he should say farewell to the American people. He didn't want to just make a speech; he wanted to do something more useful. He finally decided to write out some of his thoughts, ideas, and suggestions for the future of the country, and have them printed so that many people could read them. Using the speech James Madison had written for him four years earlier, and with the help of his longtime friends, Alexander Hamilton and John Jay, Washington put together a long piece of writing which, he said, was the "warnings of a parting friend to the American people." He gave this to the publisher of a Philadelphia newspaper, and it was printed in the newspaper on September 18, 1796, as "Washington's Farewell Address."

Washington's main purpose in preparing the Farewell Address was to make it absolutely clear to everyone that he would not run for president again. But he also wanted to explain to everyone why he had done some of the things he had done as president, and he very much wanted to offer his advice and ideas about the future of the nation. He urged all Americans to always obey the Constitution, which served as a protection to all of them; he urged them to work to see that education was available to everyone, because education made people desire freedom and liberty; he warned against becoming too friendly with some nations and unfriendly with others, because this could easily lead to war. He also warned against the danger of political parties becoming such bitter enemies that differences among them could divide, or even destroy, the nation.

Washington did not take part in the election campaign for the next president, although he hoped that his vice-president, John Adams, would win. Washington felt that Adams, who was a Federalist, would try to do most of the things Washington himself would try to do. Adams did win.

Final Days

George and Martha Washington went happily back home to Mount Vernon, and Washington spent the next year mainly just taking care of the plantation. As time went on, all the attacks and all the criticism of things he had done were forgotten. Once again, he seemed to have the respect of all the American people.

In 1799, Federalist politicians who feared that a Democratic-Republican would be elected president, wanted Washington to run for president again, as a Federalist. Washington let them know that he would not consider it, mainly because he did not think that at his age he could take the hard work and pressure.

In December of that year, Washington caught a bad cold which quickly got worse. In the dark hours of the morning of December 14 he began to shake with chills, and his throat was so sore he could barely speak. Three doctors were called in during the day, but despite everything they could do, it became more and more difficult for Washington to breathe. Late that afternoon, he told them in a whisper, "You had better not take any more trouble about me, but let me go off quietly. I cannot last long." At about

Statue of Washington in Virginia, a copy of which stands in London, capital of the country whose army Washington defeated

ten o'clock that night, he said that he felt himself going, and asked those around him to have his body put in his family tomb at Mount Vernon. When they assured him this would be done, he whispered, " 'Tis well." Moments later he was dead.

Most of those who knew George Washington well felt that he was truly a wise, good, and great man. He was not, apparently, a brilliant thinker, but he thought things over slowly and carefully, and once he made up his mind he stuck to his decision. He was honest and fair and unfalteringly brave. He did have faults; for one thing, he was absolutely determined to get every bit of anything he felt was owed to him, whether it was money, promotion, or respect. But he was always unselfishly willing to give up his private life and comfort to serve his country and his fellow citizens, if he felt they truly wanted him and he could do the best job for them. He was a good general, both as a fighting commander and as an administrator who did everything he could to improve things for the men under his command. And the part he played in overseeing the birth of the Constitution and then in helping make the Constitution work, as the first president to serve under it, was of tremendous importance. Shortly after Washington's death, Henry Lee, one of the men who had served as a general under him during the Revolutionary War, said that Washington was "first in war, first in peace, and first in the hearts of his countrymen"—meaning that Washington was a great general, a great statesman, and a man who was greatly admired and respected by everyone. There seems no doubt but that most Americans agreed.

For Further Reading

The Battle of Yorktown. American Heritage, 1968.

Busoni, Rafaello. *The Youngest General: A Story of Lafayette.* Knopf, 1949.

Clapp, Patricia. *I'm Deborah Sampson: A Soldier in the War of the Revolution.* Lothrop, 1977.

Clarke, Clorinda. *The American Revolution, 1775–83: A British View.* McGraw-Hill, 1967.

Eaton, Jeanette. *Leader by Destiny.* Harcourt, 1938.

Forbes, Esther. *Johnny Tremain.* Houghton Mifflin, 1943.

Foster, Genevieve. *George Washington's World.* Scribner, 1941.

Frankenburg, Robert. *George Washington, Leader of the People.* Follett, 1951.

The French and Indian Wars. American Heritage, 1962.

Hall-Quest, Olga. *From Colony to Nation: With Washington and His Army in the War for Independence.* Dutton, 1966.

Streeter, Sherry. *Rebecca's War*. Warne, 1972.

Walker, Nedda. *Martha, Daughter of Virginia: The Story of Martha Washington*. Dutton, 1947.

Welsh, Douglas. *The Revolutionary War*. Galahad, 1982.

Williams, Selma R. *Fifty-Five Fathers: The Story of the Constitutional Convention*. Dodd, Mead, 1970.

Wilson, Hazel. *The Story of Anthony Wayne*. Grosset & Dunlap, 1953.

Index